To Lead Is to Serve

To Lead Is to Serve

Brother René Stockman

© 2009 Novalis Publishing Inc.

Cover: Blair Turner
Layout: Audrey Wells

Business Offices:
Novalis Publishing Inc.
10 Lower Spadina Avenue, Suite 400
Toronto, Ontario, Canada
M5V 2Z2

Novalis Publishing Inc.
4475 Frontenac Street
Montréal, Québec
Canada H2H 2S2

Phone: 1-800-387-7164
Fax: 1-800-204-4140
E-mail: books@novalis.ca

www.novalis.ca

Library and Archives Canada Cataloguing in Publication

Stockman, René
 To lead is to serve / René Stockman.

ISBN 978-2-89646-128-8

 1. Leadership--Religious aspects--Christianity. 2. Christian leadership. I. Title.

BV4597.53.L43 S75 2009   253   C2009-900951-X

Printed in Canada.

All rights reserved. No part of this publication may be reproduced, stored in a retrieval system, or transmitted in any form, or by any means, electronic, mechanical, photocopying, recording, or otherwise, without the written permission of the publisher.

We acknowledge the financial support of the Government of Canada through the Book Publishing Industry Development Program (BPIDP) for our publishing activities.

5 4 3 2 1   13 12 11 10 09

Contents

Introduction 7

1. No Leadership Without Spirituality 11
2. Knowing Whom We Serve 19
3. The Importance of Role Models 27
4. I Am the Organization 37
5. A Package with Precious Contents 47
6. The Leader's Ability to Adapt 57
7. The Ethics of Leadership 65
8. I Am Only Human 73
9. Christ-inspired Leadership 83

Introduction

I am often asked to give talks about leadership. When I first began doing these talks, I would look for adequate definitions or interesting views on this topic. Certain issues cropped up time and again in my research. Most contemporary authors agreed that there was a difference between management techniques on the one hand and leadership style on the other.

I shared many of their views, especially the following point: leadership style is given shape by one's successes, by one's failures, and by the way people react to it. One acquires the capacity to lead a team or run an institution only gradually. I knew this instinctively. Having fulfilled managerial tasks for more than 25 years, I had developed a leadership style based on my own personality. When I was still a fairly young Brother, I was appointed head of a section of a hospital for children with serious developmental disabilities. All of a sudden, I found myself in charge of a group of educators, child care workers, and other staff who were all several years older than I. Despite my lack of experience, I did well in the job. What was the reason for my success? I do not really know. Was it the fact that, with my educational background, I was the most qualified person for that job? Was it because several of my fellow heads of section were real role models for me, or because my superior and the head of the institution encouraged me every day? All I know for certain is that I fulfilled my task as enthusiastically as possible, that I was always the first one to arrive in the morning and the last one to leave at the end of the day, and that I treated the members of the staff with respect.

When I left to resume my studies, the group wished me good luck and expressed the hope of meeting me again, for I had been a "good, stern, and correct leader." I have never forgotten those words, even when I was given a new leadership task that involved broader responsibilities. I was almost always one of the youngest to become manager or leader; usually, I succeeded someone who was older than I. Since then, when I have taken leave of a team, I have frequently been told that I was "good, stern, and correct."

I cannot claim that I was the best leader. But I have always tried to let the good prevail and to remember whom I was serving.

Introduction

"Stern" may have negative connotations, but for me it was necessary to be stern. I have high standards for a reason: I lead teams of people who dedicate themselves to those who do not have the same opportunities or the same capacity to defend themselves or stand up for their own rights. It is my responsibility to defend the more vulnerable – to be their spokesperson, their advocate.

Being "correct" has to do with my strong sense of justice and my desire for the truth. To always tell the truth and to be just: these were the most sacred values that my mother and father passed on to me, and I am grateful to them for this great gift.

In this essay, I wish to reflect on leadership while taking into account my own experiences so far. I feel lucky to have been given the opportunity to lead other people. Leaders ought to feel invited to live their own ideals, to realize them, and to become examples for others. This is an innovative approach to leadership. Hence my gratitude for being given new mandates at the heart of the Brothers of Charity, the religious congregation to which I belong. Today, I serve the congregation as Superior General. My mission entails that I am active on an international, global level. In fact, I am writing this introduction on the banks of Lac-Poulin, in Québec, Canada, where the Canadian Brothers own a summer house and where I am relaxing after directing a retreat. Next week I will pay my annual visit to Rwanda, where my confreres will expect me to give them spiritual guidance as well as professional, technical, and structural advice. The following week I will be in Rome to lead a training session on spirituality for a group of young Brothers from Asia and Africa who are preparing for their perpetual vows. During part of the session, I will discuss the spirituality involved in leading people. I hope I will succeed in modelling the ideals I uphold.

1

No Leadership Without Spirituality

When reflecting on or talking about leadership today, it is impossible not to refer to prominent personalities from the world of spirituality. Check any list of books on leadership and you will find quotations from or examples of Eastern mystics whose doctrines can direct modern-day leaders; from the wisdom of the desert fathers who give numerous guidelines for managers; from the rules of important monastic orders, which contain a considerable number of instructions for their leaders, and which, provided that they are updated, may be useful to contemporary managers and leaders; from the apostles; or even from Jesus himself.

So-called management gurus offer countless expensive courses on management techniques. Yet when managers are asked about the secret to successful leadership, most of them reply that although management techniques were useful to a certain extent, something else played a far more important role. In other words, being a good leader involves more than using a few techniques.

This is a remarkable evolution. It seems as though we have entered a new era of leadership – or, rather, we are rediscovering the ancient models whereby groups of people were led rather than managed. The new jargon is made up of typically "spiritual" words: charisma, zeal, motivation, spirituality. One of the keys to successful leadership is having a spiritual life to boost one's professional abilities. I would add that real leadership cannot take root if the humus of a spiritual life is lacking.

It comes down to continually rediscovering our points of reference and refining our motives. We tend to forget what our work is all about when we become engrossed in it. If we neglect to focus on the big picture, we may fail to notice when our behaviour is driven by inappropriate motives.

I have the advantage of being a religious, which means that, as part of what I might call my profession, I am invited to remain alert to the spiritual dimension of life. Every day, I must examine my conscience and pray with the Bible. Every day, I celebrate the Eucharist and open my mind to the grace of God. I live among like-minded people who also lead a spiritual life. They are the humus in which my life has taken root and from which I draw my daily energy. Even in the context of my work I am invited to take the message of the Gospel seriously! I am called to imitate Jesus, who looked after the poor, the sick, and the sinful. In other words, I am privileged in that I can integrate that spiritual dimension in both my private life and my professional activities.

I often think of all the managers who bear responsibility in banks and other large corporations in which so many and such diverse interests are at stake. These managers function in a merciless world of fierce competitors and shareholders whose only desire is to make ever bigger profits. In addition, managers in these areas of business must look after their families and fulfill a number of other social functions. When do they get time to replenish their souls, to draw up a daily agenda that leaves enough time to consume food for the spirit? No matter how busy we are, a spiritual life is essential if we wish to continuously refine and purify our views on the world and on humankind.

What are my views on humankind and on the world? And how do I try to live up to those ideal views? Each of us must have time to grapple with these questions. Our answers reveal how we wish to give to our ideal in life and in the world that we are trying to build. When we put these ideals into practice on the job, they may grow into a general view on life itself. On the basis of that incarnated view, we can guide other individuals and give direction, bearing witness to our own convictions while respecting each person's freedom.

People must determine for themselves the sources from which they wish to draw. For me, that source is the Christian faith in which I was raised, and which has determined my choices in life. Others follow another philosophy or religion, but, to my mind, it is impossible to live without any kind of orientation. Our religion or philosophy gives direction to our actions as well as to our way of leading other people. It is Jesus Christ who appears to me continually and invites me to follow his example in the course of my life and in my dealings with other people.

Every spiritual life contains this double dimension. Our spiritual life gives direction to our life as such, in relation to the divinity we worship, who invites us to live a life of high moral standards. It also determines the way we deal with the people and the world around us. Our fascination with God goes hand in hand with our morality. Our love of life – our own life and the lives of others – is a reflection of the love we receive from and give to God. Religion is always a reflection of a service to humankind. Our spiritual life drives us into the heart of this world and invites us to deal with it in a more spiritual way. Even if we adhere to the strictest and most rigid desert spirituality, it can become fruitful only if we engage in activities in the world. A spirituality that requires us to withdraw fully from the world or to seek solace in a virtual world is a false spirituality.

Our spirituality constantly invites us to assess our actions. Orientation is the process by which we give direction to our life at the very beginning. Over time, we must assess or update our orientation. As we assess, we look back upon the direction of our life and ask whether the direction we chose was the right one, or whether we strayed from the path of life we chose. The redirection that comes after the assessment is a reorientation of our actions towards the ideal to which we strove.

This terminology may sound very managerial, but it is pertinent only when it is connected to our lives as a whole. It loses its pertinence when it is disconnected from our views on the world and on humankind. That is why I support proper training for managers, as long as it has a sound spiritual foundation. If that is not the case, management remains an empty box. Worse, it may become an accumulation of techniques and procedures that may prompt managers to consider the organization to be more important than its members. This is the story of the soulless company, of bureaucratic government structures, of policy based only on the determination and implementation of procedures.

The above description is all too common these days. We are all familiar with managers who get excited only about figures and about the legal rules that are relevant to their company or organization. Their theoretical knowledge is a mask behind which they hide their incompetence in dealing with their employees in a humane fashion.

Equally familiar are the civil servant types who feel safe only when there are procedures to be followed and standard forms to be filled out, and who get all excited whenever a new procedure is added to the list – that is, until the procedures and forms take on a life of their own. I remember such an incident in Congo. In order to obtain a special visa to visit the mining region of the Kasai, I had to present myself at no fewer than thirteen different offices! At each one, the civil servants kept busy filling out more and more forms. Ultimately, I obtained my visa thanks to a personal intervention from the Minister of the Interior himself, whose daughter was a trainee at one of our institutes, and also thanks to a bribe. In the meantime, I had lost a whole day in Kinshasa. Someone told me afterwards that Congo had inherited its bureaucracy from the Belgians. (As a Belgian, I was not proud of this!)

Then there are leaders who are demagogues. They manage to mobilize entire groups, even entire peoples, for their cause, but, in most cases, eventually lead them towards their own decline. Their leadership and mission may be based on certain views of humankind and of the world, but these views often boil down to a desire for the elite to seize power. The advantaging of one group coincides with the disadvantaging or even elimination of others. Ultimately, those who benefit most are the leader and a small entourage of protégés who prefer personal gain to the well-being of the community. For some reason, history continues to summon forth such leaders, who always seem to succeed in imposing their views on other people – at least for a time.

As leaders, we must learn from such problematic examples. We must continue to test our views and our convictions against the solid source of our spirituality, and discuss them with people who can judge them objectively.

Leaders must not surround themselves with "yes-men" or "yes-women" who always agree with them because of the advantages involved in slavishly following their leader. Every leader needs people in his or her entourage who are not afraid to be critical, to oppose certain ideas. Leaders should continue to gather around them people who deem the common good more important than personal gain.

In terms of the spiritual life, leaders need a spiritual guide who helps them distinguish what is good. That person should be the one who holds up the mirror in front of the leader and who, kindly but firmly, invites the leader to look into it. The spiritual guide reveals the truth about the leader's personality and actions. Leaders need that mirror in which they see their own reflection in order to orientate their actions consistently according to the truth.

As leaders, therefore, we must make sure that our leadership is rooted firmly in the humus of a religion or a philosophy upon which we can develop our personal spirituality. But it is not enough to attend a training session every now and then, or to read one book per year on the subject. It must become a part of our life. We must make time to replenish our spirit.

Real leaders should be, above all, spiritual people who are capable of transcending personal interests. They should assess and give direction to their leadership on the basis of their personal spirituality. To accomplish that task, they will require help from outsiders who tell them the truth about their life and about their actions, as though they were holding a mirror before the leader. It is dangerous to listen to people who say "yes" only because it is in their personal interest to do so. A true spirituality that we share with and profess to others is what ought to drive us as leaders.

2

Knowing Whom We Serve

A manager in Ireland once told me the following story:

On weekdays, I have to work my way through documents of all kinds for I have to make sure that the institute survives financially. As a member of the board, it is my task to watch over this and I know that my vote counts when important decisions have to be taken. But in order to prevent myself from taking decisions on a purely economic and financial level, I invite a resident to join me for a game of golf every Saturday. He then has to remind me about whom I actually work for. I find that it is important to remember whom one is serving.

This story moved me very deeply when I first heard it. To a large extent, it has determined my leadership style. For it is indeed dangerous to settle in our office and lose sight of the people for whom the organization was originally created and for whom it continues to exist. Every organization has its clients. They either purchase goods or benefit from a certain type of service. As leaders, we should know who those clients are and whether they are satisfied with the products or services that are offered to them – not only for purely economic reasons, but also because it proves that our intentions towards the clients are honest and respectable.

The Irish manager's story encouraged me to make time to meet with clients. As head of a school, I would teach a few hours per week to stay informed about what occupied the students' minds. I would also set aside certain moments of the day for students who wanted to talk to me.

As director of a hospital, I would try to visit a number of wards every day. I would make those rounds after hours to give myself the time and opportunity to meet patients, to listen to their stories and requests.

Later on, when I became responsible for a whole group of facilities, I tried to visit each facility on a regular basis. In the mornings, I would attend a meeting with the board of directors; in the afternoon, I would visit the various wards or other areas to meet patients or residents. I felt it was important to make eye contact and to let them question me about my role in the organization, because they are the ones for whom I worked, the ones I served.

I still find it extremely important to stay in touch with the people at the ground level, to visit and meet confreres in their own environment, and to spend time with the people they care for and educate.

I must admit that I have serious doubts sometimes about the way certain managers fulfill their function these days. They rush from one meeting to another, spending half their time off the premises to attend conferences, take part in workshops, and negotiate with other facilities and organizations. What has become of spontaneous encounters with their own employees and clients? I fear that the few spare moments during which such encounters might occur are the first to be reserved for other appointments when the weekly schedule is drawn up, the first to be cut back when seemingly more important matters arise. I suspect that those managers will discover in due course that, although they still talk about clients, they no longer know who those clients actually are.

It is therefore essential to preserve two sacred moments in the weekly schedule: a visit to a place where we can meet clients, and a blank spot on the schedule for unexpected encounters. We must meet with members of the staff, with the people who are responsible for referring clients and patients, and with the clients themselves. These encounters are crucial if we wish to stay in touch with what happens at the ground level of the organization and what occupies the minds of the people at the bottom of the hierarchy. How can we make realistic decisions if we no longer know the concerns and the everyday realities of our staff or clients? It is the unique face of each individual client that influences us to take his or her wishes and remarks into account when making decisions that will affect him or her. If we neglect to spend time looking at individual faces, other parameters – financial and economic parameters, organizational parameters, logistic parameters – will determine the decision-making process. While these are important factors, and we must keep them in our sights, they must never constitute the sole arguments of our decisions. Leaders should ask themselves which of their organization's aims is key to the decision-making process. A good leader should be capable of listening attentively and with an open mind to all arguments, then weigh them carefully, and compare them with the first and only objective of the organization.

Effective leaders make time to reflect regularly on the central objective of their organization. They need the advice and aid of a diverse group of specialists in order to guard against becoming overly engrossed in managerial tasks. If they are obliged to occupy their mind with too many details and small matters due to a lack of competent assistants, leaders will not have enough time left to concentrate on the essence of their work.

It is tempting for those who have ultimate responsibility for an organization to meddle in affairs connected to their own specialty – to give priority to such matters or to devote comparatively more attention to them when it comes to making decisions. Yet leaders should be capable of transcending their own discipline and should pay more attention to less familiar disciplines, in which they are less accomplished. Doing so will help leaders to attain a certain balance and to maintain focus. Today, much attention is focused on quality. Manuals on the subject of quality care are published, quality labels are awarded, and companies employ quality-control experts. The fact that companies, schools, and institutions are paying ever more attention to quality is a positive development. However, we need to answer two questions in regard to quality: what sort of quality are we talking about, and what motivates the leader to be concerned about quality?

Many theories about quality have been developed. Although they may sound impressive, they have very little to do with what really matters in life. They deal with minor phenomena but ignore central values. We can speak about quality in a meaningful way, and address the matter of the quality of the product or service that clients receive, only if we base our reflection on our view of humankind. What type of human do we wish to promote? What values should be fostered to that purpose? Our deeper reflections on humankind need to be based on thorough knowledge of humankind. Our theorizing needs to coincide with some practical thinking. Only then can we say anything meaningful about humankind, about what is precious, and what represents real quality of life. Let this be the start of every activity that aims to influence or improve the quality of the care and guidance we offer.

It is tempting to measure quality purely on the basis of a number of conditions related to exterior characteristics, and to conclude, when those conditions are fulfilled, that we have nothing more to worry about. However, it might well be that those measurable factors tell very little about real life, and possibly even ignore it. All leaders should give the highest priority to quality, but they should not be satisfied with a measuring tool developed in some laboratory entrusted to a so-called quality co-ordinator.

Measuring instruments can be useful, and quality co-ordinators may do a good job – but only if the organization's leaders have first reflected on what quality ought to stand for, and the quality co-ordinator's results are taken seriously and read attentively. Leaders who talk about quality because it is fashionable, or because they want to put a quality label on their stationery and at the building's entrance, prove the necessity of guarding against improper motives. It's something like drawing up a mission statement. How many mission statements have been drawn up in the manager's office on a Friday afternoon, with no other intention than to be able to hang a framed statement on a wall somewhere? A strong mission statement is rooted in a reflection that involves as many staff as possible and a continuous process of sensitization and evaluation. The mission statement raises a question concerning the organization's ultimate objective, a question whose answer should satisfy the client. When meeting clients and raising the question about quality, leaders must remain mindful of that mission statement.

Quality and mission become operational only when they focus on the client, and when their foundation is a profound reflection on humankind and on the way we wish to influence quality in a positive way. A director of one of our psychiatric centres once told me that he often asked himself whether he would want his father to be hospitalized and treated at his psychiatric centre, should his father need care. Such considerations should be our touchstone for quality.

The only right way for managers to evaluate their organization is to become personally involved. For then the clients become people whom managers really know, and for whom only the best is good enough. There is no need for us to wait until our fathers become clients to become personally involved with clients. After all, our clients are our true employers.

3

The Importance of Role Models

In a recent publication on leadership, several prominent leaders and managers were asked to name the people who had inspired them the most and to give the reason. Some of the names that were mentioned most often were Gandhi, Martin Luther King, Winston Churchill, and John F. Kennedy: great people who played significant roles in the history of the world, who left their mark. As I read the publication, I started to think about people who have played, and still play, an important role in my life and who have influenced my leadership style.

Two groups of people help shape our actions: people we have met personally, and figures from history. It is good to cultivate both groups, because they complement one another. They inspire us through the things they do and the things they say. Mindful of the saying "actions speak louder than words," we understand well the importance of models.

At the age of twelve, I was sent to a school run by Brothers. Having come from a small village school, I had trouble finding my way around the buildings at first. The headmaster himself made me feel comfortable and accepted with a single gesture. He had a habit of walking around at playtime and addressing pupils personally. Although he seemed to be a real authority figure, someone to fear, he was very friendly to us. A remarkable combination! During the first few days of school, he would approach me, pat me on the back, and ask, "René, are you feeling a bit more at ease yet?" I was astonished. He knew my name — me, the new boy — among 80 others, and he knew what was troubling me.

At lunch, I would see that same headmaster serve pupils in the refectory, wearing a grey dustcoat over his black habit. He would always use our first name when he spoke to us — sometimes kindly, sometimes to correct us, sometimes to express concern. When he would whistle for silence, we would be quiet as mice, and when he began to pray in his hoarse voice, none of us dared look up. That Brother was my headmaster for six years. Many years later, when he had severe dementia, I was the only person he still seemed to recognize in a flash. He still called me by my name.

The features that struck me about that man who served as a leader in many contexts for over half a century were a winning combination: a healthy degree of aloofness that is required of persons who exercise authority, personal involvement, and a high degree of service.

When I was still a fairly young Brother, I met and got to know an elderly confrere who had spent many years in the highest echelons of the congregation. At the time of our acquaintance, he was teaching youngsters who were preparing for their exams at the central examination board; he spent the rest of his time compiling texts for a magazine. Here was a 75-year-old who still knew how to hold the attention of a group of seventeen-year-olds, and who had taught himself to offer leadership to nurses through the publication of his magazine. What struck me about that man was his capacity to adapt constantly to new situations; his decision to continue to study so he could better serve others; and his willingness to do any kind of service, as long as it fitted with his vocation in life. On his deathbed, he asked me to make sure that his magazine continued to be published. Not only did I take responsibility for the magazine, but also I tried to imitate his zeal as a student and his willingness to adapt to new situations.

Some of my superiors put me on the right track through their words and actions. For example, the superior of my first apostolate visited me every day. He seemed to have all the time in the world to walk around the institute. Some people criticized him for "wasting" time. Yet he was the one who taught me the importance of maintaining informal contact with one's staff and clients, in a variety of situations. How effective is the manager who meets with staff members only in stressful and negative situations?

Yet another superior made a profound impression on me with this saying: "No greater injustice than equality!" Later, he explained what he meant. According to him, certain general rules had to be respected, but in some cases, in the interests of a particular individual, a leader was justified in bending those rules. Strong leaders are those who can make such wise distinctions.

One superior told me that before tackling a problem, he would always read a comic book, because it left him with a fresh and relaxed mind. Still another knew very well how to put his own words and actions into perspective, thanks to a rich sense of humour. "Never take yourself too seriously, but always keep your sense of humour," he would say.

And then there was the generosity of the one who would, quite willingly, organize a party for us, and the forgiveness of another who, quietly, would turn a page

The Importance of Role Models

and declare a subject closed. We were called upon to place a high priority on hospitality. The generous superior confided to me that he knew he contributed much to the atmosphere in the group. If necessary, he would bring out an extra bottle of wine to show hospitality and encourage us to enjoy our fellowship.

One of my professors encouraged me to continue my studies, to do a doctorate because he thought that with this degree I might be better able to serve the congregation. He was yet another example of a leader who had the gift of uttering exactly the right word of encouragement at the right time. I also remember him because he always kept his appointments, and because although he had contacts at the highest levels of politics, he also remembered the receptionist's and cleaner's names.

I have come to the conclusion that good leaders are often paradoxical figures. Their authority wins them respect and their friendliness puts people at ease. They are totally committed to their cause, but are nevertheless prepared to start something new with just as much enthusiasm. They make sure that people obey the rules, but will sometimes bend them or make exceptions in the interests of the individual. They are earnest, but still have a sense of humour. They are good at correcting others, but even better at encouraging them. They are people whom we meet on our path of life and who inspire us;

they are living role models who complete the puzzle of our own life by providing the missing pieces.

Figures from the past can also give direction or become models for the type of leader we would like to become. Countless men and women in history serve as role models, inspiring us to push past our limits, try new things, and stay true to ourselves. One such person for me is Peter Joseph Triest, who founded my congregation, the Brothers of Charity, in 1807. He formulated his mission during his first public appearance, after having lived in hiding for five years. "I am to be a good example for you. I am to teach you, and I am to serve you," he said.

Leaders should realize that their teachings will remain ineffective if they do not live up to them. As we know from experience, words are cheap and meaningless when they are not followed by actions. Living up to what we say we do, becoming what we claim to be: that is what leadership is all about. Add the need to serve others, and we have an adequate profile of the primary requirements of any leader.

Seeing our leadership as a form of service to others, and continuing to see it as such, is what being a leader boils down to. How quickly most leaders forget that they are doing people a service. Peter Joseph Triest did more than put service at the heart of his mission. Over the next 30 years of his life, he lived up to his mission consistently. Throughout his life, he aimed to serve other

The Importance of Role Models

people. In fact, his life was one long attempt to please and to serve. Such an orientation led him to go very far in his preference for the poor, and made him incredibly brave and inventive.

Triest always had the courage to start all over again, and was never deterred by opposition or difficult circumstances. And he was always able to arrive at solutions despite such opposition and difficult circumstances. The secret of Triest's success was that wonderful combination of enormous faith in God and zest for his own work.

He demonstrated with grace how heavy responsibilities do not need to prevent us from looking after a neighbour, and how they do not relieve us of the obligation of paying attention to details. Although he had overall responsibility for relief for the poor in Ghent, he would describe meticulously how patients had to be nursed. He understood that love of one's neighbour does not exclude professionalism. Rather, such professionalism is essential if that love is to be expressed in something more than beautiful words. Triest believed in structure, in organization, in rules and regulations, on condition that they were developed in the interests of the people in the care of his Sisters and Brothers.

Triest belonged to the school of Vincentian spirituality – his initiatives resemble those of Vincent de Paul. Triest also combined two aspects of service: taking personal care of the poor, and organizing such care. He proclaimed that religion must always result in fraternal love, that a spiritual life was essential to a life of service, and that the poor were our masters. In describing good leadership, Triest and St. Vincent both spoke of Christ, who came into this world as a shepherd.

Christ was the One who spoke the word, who taught us, who called himself "the way, the truth, and the life." He was a leader who preached consciously, who translated God's message for the people around him, who spoke the words by which he himself lived. He was also the one who forgave sinners, cured the sick, and healed people spiritually and physically. He was a leader who would call a sin by its proper name, but who was willing to give the sinner another chance. He gave people hope even when their situations looked desperate. He was, above all, a servant leader who washed his disciples' feet as a symbol of the usual expectations being turned upside down: the very next day, he would sacrifice his own life so that countless others should live.

For many people, Christ is the ultimate role model for life. Many leaders see him in this light as well. Christ was a leader who called himself a shepherd. He knew his sheep by name, and was willing to leave the flock in order to find one lost soul.

The Gospel is full of phrases and stories that can inspire our leadership. He is the opposite of all rulers of the world by putting all emphasis on service (Matthew 20:25-26). With his view of the Kingdom of God, he develops a new world image and invites everyone to experience the spirit of the Beatitudes, even in leadership (Mark 5:3-10). Christ also introduces a completely new scale of values in which love, justice, and forgiveness have absolute priority (Mark 12:29-31; Matthew 20:1-16; Matthew 18:21-23). When we spend time reading and pondering the Word of God, our leadership is renewed, enriched, reoriented. Christ is the ultimate role model for Christians. With him, we are in good company.

4

I Am the Organization

Some leaders identify themselves with the organization that they represent. I still remember being impressed by the former French president, Charles de Gaulle, who concluded all of his speeches with the words "La France, c'est moi." He was a leader who felt at one with his country. By claiming this bond, he appealed to his fellow citizens to commit themselves to the well-being of the whole nation as well. We can dedicate ourselves to a cause only when we own it and identify with it. Yet it takes time to know an organization, to learn about a certain cause, to grow into it.

We must become familiar with the organization's history, its founders, the story of its beginnings. During my novitiate, the early years of preparing to be a Brother, I realized how important it was to study the history of our religious congregation as part of my spiritual formation. It is with good reason that the Second Vatican Council encouraged religious communities to move in two directions: in the direction of the past, back to their roots, to learn about the charism or gift of the founder; and then in the direction of the present, the so-called *aggiornamento*, or bringing up to date, to translate that original charism faithfully for today.

In the entrance hall of the headquarters of a Belgian supermarket chain stands a dogcart – a two-wheeled open carriage. This cart symbolized the beginning of that supermarket chain 75 years ago. The founder, now an elderly man, loved to tell how, as a young boy, he went around buying goods for people and delivering them to their homes using the cart. He also supplied a small number of shops. He worked from early in the morning until late at night. Many years later, after his grandchildren had taken over the company, he continued to visit several convents to supply them with food every week, the way he had done in the beginning. It was always a pleasure to listen to his stories about the old days. The dogcart had become a symbol of hard work and his service to customers. The old founder stayed involved in his work by keeping busy. He was a living witness of what the company stood for. Sometimes he would complain that his grandchildren were much more concerned about company shares than about the company itself. It was his way of saying that he was not entirely satisfied with how identified they were with the company. Identifying ourselves with our organization is essential for leaders and managers.

I admit that I have my doubts about managers who so easily and so willingly change locations or even companies frequently. Do they give themselves enough time to get to know the organization, to learn to identify themselves with it?

We must allow ourselves time to really grow into a company. The introductory phase is followed by a training period. Every organization and every company has its own "smell" of home. For example, although I travel a lot, I can sense immediately when I have entered a community of my own congregation. Minute details are often responsible for the typical character of an organization, a company, or a religious community. In our case, the identifying factors may be the rhythm of the day, the way prayers are recited, the way people treat each other, and the openness of the environment. The latter characteristic must be typical of our organization; even our lay staff notice it. They tell me that the homey atmosphere at work was something they lacked at their previous employer's.

In many cases, the term "company culture" describes this phenomenon. A certain set of habits and customs has been developed through time, adding a typical colour to the organization. This culture encompasses the way people deal with one another, the typical stresses experienced in pursuing the chief mission, the way members behave towards their environment. All these characteristics are seriously influenced and determined by the organization's underlying philosophy. All of them are connected with the way the founder and the first members or staff developed the organization.

The organization culture evolves over time. Ruptures or shifts may occur, especially if long-time managers are replaced by newcomers who are not familiar with the company's history and who do not wish to learn about it, because they intend to choose another direction. Organizations that function well attest to the importance of continuity in the culture, and their leaders are incarnations of that culture. They keep the story alive, as from the very beginning, and attentively try to prolong it and bring it up to date. To return to the original source and to update that mission, which is the task that religious communities were given, is a task other organizations should fulfill as well. The dogcart as symbol of hard work and service will become even more significant, even more symbolic, once the founder has passed away. It would be a pity if the dogcart were locked away somewhere because it no longer matches the decor of the reception area! The current leaders must continue to write the story of hard work and service. They must be examples of what they expect of their employees. In other words, they must concern themselves with much more than company shares or the bottom line.

Leaders as incarnations of an organization's culture – this is one way to describe how leaders are to identify themselves with their organization. It takes time to develop this approach. My own experience is a good example. I have had the opportunity to live and work among Brothers for many years. Getting to know them and listening to their stories were important steps in the process of learning the culture of the congregation, which they unknowingly taught me. Eventually, I felt completely at home. I felt a sense of unity with my confreres, and I could paraphrase de Gaulle and say, "I am the congregation."

Only when we have gone through this rigorous process are we ready to become leaders. When we are capable of being an example of that culture, we become a reference for the organization and can speak for the organization.

What about organizations that attract newcomers to assume ultimate responsibility immediately? These candidates may well be good managers – good leaders, even – but they lack something fundamental: a deep understanding of the place. Without it, they cannot become the heart of the organization. The new leader must make serious efforts to become familiar with the history and culture of the group if he or she is to be its heart.

Leaders who identify themselves with the organization completely are usually prepared to devote much time to the organization – all their time, in fact. I realize that this is not a popular opinion. We tend to distinguish clearly between our working hours and our spare time. It is supposedly impossible to maintain a healthy psychological balance if we don't make this distinction.

However, I am convinced that we can attain a healthy psychological balance when we devote ourselves completely to our task and become engrossed in it – provided we do not lose ourselves in it. Finding time to reflect on my task at the heart of the organization helps me to avoid working too much. It all comes down to finding that balance, that inner peace, that sense of well-being, precisely because one feels so involved in the organization. When we are away from work, when we are relaxing or doing other things, we are often still discerning or integrating thoughts, ideas, or decisions and dreaming about new initiatives. Although these may be taking place on the back burner, far from our laptop, cell phone or office, they are a valuable part of our work efforts. Perhaps people who make a strict distinction between their working hours and their spare time do so because they consider their task a burden and wish to prevent their negativity from affecting their spare time.

When we can identify ourselves with the organization, we quite willingly consider that organization as a part of ourselves. Then we do not only work for it, but actually live for it. Those who are devoted to the organization they work for must not be considered workaholics or slaves to their work. Identification is the result of a decision made freely and has nothing to do with slavery. Yet we must also take care of our health in the interest of our mission.

Every leader needs to make time to relax, to reflect, to evaluate, and even to reorient. When we are always preoccupied and don't find time to evaluate our preoccupation, we run the risk of wearing ourselves out completely. Plan a number of moments throughout the week, the month, the year, during which you can approach the organization in a different way: meditation, reflection, preparation, evaluation. It might well be the most fruitful time you spend on the organization. It is not always in meetings or negotiations that we manage the organization in the best possible way. A day spent in a quiet and peaceful environment may enrich our leadership, or help us to identify ourselves with the organization even more closely.

At the time when I was responsible for the facilities of my congregation, I made a habit of spending one long weekend per month at an abbey to prepare talks, to read, and to reflect on the organization. I always returned with renewed strength and with my own resources replenished: I felt relaxed and found new energy to devote myself to the organization.

Admittedly, I cannot speak on behalf of leaders who have a family and who sometimes have difficulty dedicating themselves to the organization without neglecting their families. While I don't have a family, I do have a religious community. I have sometimes experienced that tension between the work that we call apostolate and the community. The problem was always the same: the Brothers expected certain things from me that I could not do on account of my mission. But we always managed to solve the problem, thanks to open conversation and negotiation. Mutual understanding was the solution. The same may be true for families. Encouraging family members to take an interest in the ups and downs of the organization allows the family to have a positive influence on leadership. Also, family relationships are a wonderful training ground for leaders: the values learned in the family cannot help but be brought to the organization. Those who take time to grow with their family tend to be balanced and effective leaders.

Personal involvement with an organization does not mean feeling depressed when business falters or feeling euphoric when things are going well. It is the leader's task to strive for a certain degree of stability, so he or she can cope with a range of issues and problems. In other words, do everything with saintly restlessness and, at the same time, with saintly indifference. We should indeed be restless when business is shaky or staff performance is disappointing, but we cannot allow these developments to affect our peace of mind. Even when we identify ourselves with the organization, our life always amounts to more than the organization.

Those who believe in God feel sustained by God, who continues to support them, even when the ground beneath their feet is giving way. This is the kind of faith that we should wish to transmit to the organization. The image of the captain who is the last to leave the sinking ship is appropriate here. Does he do so because he believes that the ship can still be saved, or because he feels responsible for the ship's most important load, the crew? This image applies to organizations as well. Leaders continue to believe in the cause because it has become a part of them. And they love their employees because employees represent the heart of the organization.

5

A Package with Precious Contents

Leading a team, group, or organization consists primarily of two tasks: taking care of the structure, and taking care of the contents. The activities leaders undertake must always demonstrate those two components; ideally, there should be a healthy balance between them. Care for the contents comes first: formulating a mission, making sure that the objectives remain pure, and encouraging the staff to fulfill their task conscientiously. However, a group also needs a certain structure: clear agreements must be made, everyone needs to know what is expected of him or her, and all staff members have rights and obligations.

Leading a team, group, or organization means looking after a box whose contents are precious, but it also means guaranteeing that the box contains the right contents and that they are preserved and used properly.

How should we set about the task of paying attention to the contents?

We have to know what the organization is about. This point may sound obvious and even banal, but it is essential. We expect a leader to be informed about what is happening at the heart of the organization. The leader does not need to know all the details, which would be impossible, but must have at least a general idea of what has been going on. The director of a hospital must keep informed about nursing activities, about recent developments in the medical world, and about the possible consequences of certain therapies. A leader whose task is to manage the package, and who relies only on a financial and economic background, lacks an important element and runs the risk of approaching things from an incomplete perspective. I am therefore convinced that leaders must possess knowledge of the core activities of the organization, preferably on the basis of their own education, which is maintained and developed through extra training and practical experience.

As a hospital director, I was able to fall back on my basic training as a nurse. As head of a school, I could rely on my training as a teacher. As superior general of a congregation, I draw on my own religious formation. It is not always possible for managers to possess exactly the right degrees, certificates, or diplomas; where these are lacking, managers must pursue supplementary training – not only in the field of management skills, but also in relation to the core activities of the organization.

Such training can be diverse: attending lectures and workshops, participating actively in internal training initiatives, and reading specialist literature. Personally, I have learned much from having to give courses or talks. Preparing for these events forces me to read, to study, and to think. Leaders of every organization are often invited to give a talk or to provide internal training sessions. While preparing for such occasions, they must research a particular topic and develop their personal views on it. Leaders must also represent their organization to other organizations or authorities, and explain their operations. Thanks to these external catalysts, leaders are motivated to stay informed, to keep up to date, and to make time for extra training.

Indirectly, this approach is in the interests of the organization. Leaders must not lock themselves up in their own organization, convinced that all contact with external parties is a waste of energy. On the contrary, managers need to make conscious choices, ponder what is important and feasible, and always remain aware of their primary mission. One of the central tasks of managers is to formulate and embody or incarnate the mission of the organization. A mission that has been formulated correctly is the result when an organization's central mission has been tested against reality.

When it comes to leadership, theoretical knowledge, vision, and practical involvement go hand in hand. We must be able to fall back on knowledge and practical experience. If we open up to both, we are bound to witness a wonderful evolution taking place within ourselves: thanks to practical involvement, we perfect our skills and knowledge, and become specialists in various fields, developing a much broader view at the same time. To use medical terminology, we become specialists as well as general practitioners – specialists as far as the central mission of the organization is concerned, and general practitioners as far as our views on humankind and society are concerned.

A leader who is more technically skilled must make an effort to become a philosopher. Similarly, philosophers must work on their technical skills. Thus we avoid becoming one-dimensional: technicians are challenged to go beyond matter-of-fact thinking and philosophers beyond unrealistic dreaming. Leaders must find practical answers and solutions to practical problems, without losing sight of the organization's broader context. A rich combination of technical knowledge and global science, an eye for detail and for the overall situation: this is what leaders who are concerned about the contents of their mission ought to have.

Another important aspect of taking care of the contents is how we motivate our staff. On the occasion of my silver jubilee, I received a beautifully framed text from the members of my community. Here is what it says:

> If you grow weak, they will fail;
>
> If you sit down, they will lie down;
>
> If you doubt, they will despair;
>
> If you criticize, they will denounce;
>
> If you march in front, they will overtake you;
>
> If you reach out your hand, they will sacrifice their lives;
>
> If you pray, they will be saints.
>
> Be mindful of that, leader …

My confreres had often seen this text in my office. I had had a copy of it for many years, since I was a student, in fact. I cherished it because it describes so well my role as leader. Even more than words, the example we provide encourages others. For an employee, confirmation of a good effort, given at the right time by someone who lives up to what he or she believes in, can work wonders. We all remember occasions when a superior affirmed us at a difficult moment, and occasions when we affirmed a staff member at a time when that person was struggling and badly needed some encouragement. We all recall occasions when someone in a position of authority sat and heard us out, and occasions when we made time to listen to or talk about what an employee was going through. These actions do not demand spectacular management techniques, just humanity, solidarity, understanding, compassion.

In short, leading a team successfully comes down to acquiring sufficient knowledge about the central mission of the organization; embedding that knowledge in a much broader set of skills; being capable of defining the mission of the organization; conscientiously trying to fulfill that mission oneself; and dealing in a humane way with staff.

The contents of the organizational box are valuable. It is up to the leader to make sure that the package or structure that holds these contents is solid. Function specifications must be drawn up, and procedures must be elaborated.

Everyone needs to know and hold their rightful place in the organization. A lack of clarity causes uncertainty, and leads to unfulfilled actions and tasks. Members must see where they fit into the organizational chart, the visual presentation of the structure of the organization, and respect that place. They need to know whom to contact in case of a problem or a question, and who is responsible for specific functions. It comes down to developing a strict hierarchical structure in which everyone's responsibilities are clear. I do not like complicated organizational charts: they reflect organizational structures that are equally complicated. Make sure that employees do not depend on several bosses, because this setup may lead to confusion. Clarity and simplicity ought to be the key features of any organization's structure.

Employees expect to know what they are supposed to do and what their boss expects of them. If all were left to imagine for themselves what their task was, the result would be chaos.

I would like to make a distinction between function specifications and task descriptions. Ideally, it should be enough for the boss to be involved in the specification of an employee's function. The employee may then be expected to clearly understand his or her task. In this way, room for creativity is given to the staff, who can give shape to their task themselves. Some staff, however, prefer to have a clear task description. Without one, they feel insecure and cannot fulfill their task as they should. As managers, we need take these people's needs into account, adapting management to meet the needs of the staff, while always aiming to stimulate their creativity.

If a task description is necessary, keep it as brief as possible to allow for the employee's personal input. Employees are entitled to performance reviews during which they can evaluate themselves in the presence of their boss and suggest slight changes to their set of tasks. The function specification provides the frame of reference, but the way in which one fulfills one's tasks is the real test.

Every organization requires a series of procedures – descriptions of how an employee had best fulfill a certain task, and of what an employee is supposed to do in certain situations. Again, it seems advisable to limit the number of procedures. Some managers think they have things under control when everything is written down in the form of procedures. However, this kind of security is illusory; situations for which no procedure applies will invariably arise. When such situations present themselves, responsible and competent managers can react effectively.

Some employees are allergic to procedures, seeing them as the greatest obstacle to their creativity and sense of responsibility. I have experienced this kind of tension in my congregation. Some Brothers want everything to be written down in detail, while others require only the general rule of life. Most are happy with a compromise: a well-written general rule of life with a summary book of norms. Some Brothers remember the days when everything was written out in detail but ultimately became so undermined that the whole document was abandoned. We do not wish to return to that restrictive approach.

A leader, therefore, must make sure that the organization's structure serves the contents. Structures tend to take on a life of their own and to be considered more important than the content. This is how a bureaucracy comes into being. This is how the actual objectives of an organization become undermined.

As we can see, leaders must mind both the contents and the packaging. At times, the contents will demand all their attention. At other times, they will need to give more energy to the structure. The ideal is always somewhere in between. Moreover, one implies the other. A structure without contents is empty; contents without structure never achieve the ideal, the dream.

A dream becomes reality when it is embedded in an awakened world, when it enters people's everyday lives.

Leaders must continually dream and develop adequate structures in which to realize their dreams for the organization they lead.

6

The Leader's Ability to Adapt

What type of leader are you? Although this is a common question, it can be difficult to answer.

The way we lead a team has something to do with our personality, but it is also influenced by the people we lead and by the overall situation.

Our personality is like our face: unique. We are born with some basic personality traits; these are shaped by our family relationships, by life events, and by the people we meet.

If we think about how other people react and respond to us, we can estimate the impression we make. As a leader, you must be able to appraise your own personality accurately. Are you someone who reacts directly or indirectly? Someone who clings to your own views or who is easily swayed by others? Someone who is ready to take on problems as soon as they become apparent, or who prefers to tackle them in a roundabout way?

Our personality is also influenced by the values we consider important. Do you have a strong sense of justice and are you undeniably sincere, or are you prepared to accept a compromise, to turn a blind eye or even bend the truth? Are you willing to make adjustments for the personal happiness of your staff members, or is the success of the company more important than all the rest? Are you the type of person who will sacrifice your own resources for the benefit of the organization, or is the organization a way of giving shape to your personal project in life?

Leading a team also influences our personality, which indirectly determines our management style as well. Leaders might think back on their first years of being in charge. When I was the head of a school for nurses, I had to combine that function a while later with that of director of a hospital. At the school, I had learned how important it was to be clear and strict in the guidance I offered to young people. Upholding the same leadership style at the hospital, I was told that I was acting too much like a teacher, which was not appropriate in that setting. I had to find other ways of being strict and clear about things. It is true that we deal differently with adolescents than with adults. But it would be wrong to think that clarity is needed only when working with adolescents, and that all adults need is room for creativity.

Gradually, I became convinced that leadership had everything to do with adapting to different situations without betraying my own personality and values. Leadership is the art of leading a team of diverse people in the most diverse of situations, making sure that the organization's objectives are attained with the team's help. When all is said and done, people and circumstances determine our leadership style.

Some people feel more comfortable working for a leader who makes everything 100 per cent clear to them. They are like the people working on an assembly line who prefer to stick to the system of the production line. Routine allows them to spend the day without having to think too much. In the past 20 years, I visited such a factory twice. On my second visit, I could see that they had altered the production system drastically on the basis of a new philosophy. Instead of working on the assembly line, workers now had a set of tasks to fulfill in order to give them a greater sense of responsibility. The mind-numbing work was now done by robots and no longer by people. While a majority of the workers considered this change in approach to be an improvement, others did not welcome it. What one group saw as a mind-numbing routine, another experienced as a safe situation. It would have been wrong to overlook the opinion of the latter group when deciding to make the changes, but it would have been just as irresponsible to block or ignore all opportunities to upgrade people's jobs because of those few workers who opposed such an evolution. Here, the relevant question is this: to whom should a leader refer when making decisions about procedures for staff? To those who demand a completely unambiguous task description, or to those who feel that their function specifications alone give them the direction they need?

A good leader must heed both groups; in reality, even more groups exist than these two extremes. Some people require a lot of guidance, others less, but all need encouragement. A leader who believes in the growth potential of his or her staff will take care that everyone is stimulated to grow and to acquire new skills: assuming personal responsibility for an increasing number of tasks, taking more personal initiatives, becoming more involved in the organization.

We can learn something from St. Benedict, who, in the rule that he drew up for his order, encouraged the abbot to lead his monks in such a way that both the strong and the weak could thrive. To pay attention only to the weak, leaving the strong to become frustrated, or to set off with the strong, making the weak feel abandoned, are traps that every leader ought to be mindful

The Leader's Ability to Adapt

of. St. Benedict called it a sense of measure, whereby the strong are given enough guidance to be able to develop themselves, and whereby the weak are supported and encouraged to such an extent that they, too, can develop themselves. In some ways, a leader is like a teacher who is challenged to make progress with a group of students and to attain the pedagogical objectives.

I was once told a story about a teacher who got permission to postpone the holidays for several weeks so that all the students might pass their exams. Bright pupils were encouraged to become coaches to their less-gifted classmates. The stronger students were invited to use their talents on a social level and to get rid of the competitive model, where only the strong survive. How different from the "everyone for himself" model most of us have been taught! Such a model stimulates a self-centred, competitive mentality rather than a co-operative, socially responsible one.

Thank goodness that today, teamwork has become more popular in schools, and solidarity is seen as a value that cannot be overemphasized. This revised view and practice must be maintained in the workplace. Leaders, as their staff's coaches, need to develop the skill to stimulate every staff member in an adequate way, thereby encouraging the staff to support one another.

This approach requires insight into human nature and belief in people's growth potential. To illustrate this point, I return to my experience in the world of hospitals. The staff of one ward attached great importance to maintaining a homey atmosphere, but neglected some nursing techniques. Patients were cared for inadequately, medication was not administered punctually, and prescribed therapies were neglected. The staff on this ward needed to be encouraged to pay more attention to nursing tasks. One staff member was given the task of organizing supplementary training sessions, and procedures were written out. At the same time, we made sure that the family atmosphere was not lost, but was reconciled with the technical requirements. Coincidentally, on another ward, patients complained that the atmosphere was too cold, too technical. What one ward lacked abounded on another. On the second ward, we organized training sessions to improve interpersonal relationships, and convinced the head of the ward that it was equally important to pay attention to the human aspect as to procedures. In the end, we appointed an adjunct who was responsible for cultivating the human aspect.

In my current capacity as superior general, I am confronted with the enormous diversity in the fields of culture, traditions, backgrounds, and ages of our congregation. The concept of leader is understood in a completely different way in Africa and Asia than in Europe or North America. I need to adapt my approach and be aware of the different circumstances if I wish to meet the

The Leader's Ability to Adapt

expectations of my fellow Brothers. You can imagine how big a difference there is between a community that has existed for only ten years, that is full of energy and enthusiasm, and a community of elderly Brothers who have lost some of their enthusiasm. Both communities need a leader. The first needs a leader who can temper the wild enthusiasm and suggest realistic and durable objectives. The second needs a leader who can encourage members to leave the beaten track and search for new perspectives. One community will need no more than a single visit or a short talk, whereas other communities may need regular talks, sympathy, and constant guidance. It is impossible to be viewed in the same light by each individual community. Some Brothers see me as some kind of whirlwind, whereas others see me as a turtle. Some consider me to be young and inexperienced, whereas others consider my ideas old-fashioned and outdated. Other labels include conservative, rash, autocratic, progressive, too daring, not daring enough ....

Yet listening to these remarks and comments can be helpful, for they likely contain an element of truth. However, do not let yourself become disheartened or defensive. Such comments ought to stimulate one to remain flexible, for flexibility is a key characteristic of all good leaders. Flexibility must never become synonymous with arbitrariness or a laissez-faire attitude. If it did, then it would be time to step down as leader.

7

The Ethics of Leadership

When I speak to groups about leadership, I sometimes show them *Modern Times*, the 1936 Charlie Chaplin film. It is a brilliant illustration of how people can get caught in the machinery of the system. I think this film provides a good introduction to the humanity of leadership.

A discussion on leadership is always a discussion about people. We must keep affirming this point, however obvious it seems. Leaders should always focus on people and keep asking themselves whether and how they have stimulated people to attain what is good in life. These actions touch on the core question of ethics.

The organization for which we bear responsibility can have many objectives that are related to its core mission. These objectives can be economic, financial, social, therapeutic, or educational. But all must be tuned to one dominant goal: to stimulate the good in life, to make sure that each client and staff member benefits as an individual and as a member of the human family.

We can talk about ethical leadership only when concern and attention remain the leader's priorities. Such leadership is always about humankind and human well-being.

In order to remain focused on these key priorities, leaders must act virtuously. I consciously use the age-old term "virtue" because it still describes the best way to live a good life. A virtue is a value that has become a personal asset. Thanks to virtues, we succeed in bettering our own life in relationship with the lives of others. The four cardinal or primary virtues are justice, prudence, courage, and moderation. What role can they play in the life and work of a leader?

Justice means acting fairly and giving others what they are entitled to. How often we hear people complain about a lack of justice! The powerful achieve their goals thanks to their cunning. Some even seem proud to be able to exploit others. Leaders are called upon to act justly towards the people for whom they are responsible. This means adhering to working hours, offering fair wages, paying them on time, honouring the terms of employment, and ensuring that all staff members, especially the weaker ones, are respected. Justice becomes apparent as well in the use of goods, the way competitors are treated, and timely payment of taxes. In this light, practices such as transferring production lines to low-wage countries, overlooking unhealthy working conditions, tolerating child labour, and making exorbitant profits become questionable. Finally, justice has to do with the leader's own behaviour and lifestyle: income level compared to other employees' salaries; bonuses; use of company property (such as a computer and a vehicle); and how company funds are spent.

Prudence is often described as the mother of a china shop. Leaders must realize that they are dealing with people. Every mistake, every lapse in the leader's attention, may result in injury. As a trainee, I experienced the importance of prudence. Having bathed an elderly patient, I had forgotten to reinstall the rails on his bed after tucking him in. When I brought his meal an hour later, I found the man under the bed. In his confusion, he had stepped out of the bed and fallen out. Luckily, he had not hurt himself. On another occasion, I injected medication that was supposed to be taken orally. Although the colour of the ampoule should have alerted me that the medication was to be administered orally, I had not noticed it. In the end, no damage was done, but I was reminded to always be alert and prudent. One lapse in a nurse's concentration, one moment of imprudence, may have tragic consequences.

When I became a leader, I remembered these occasions when I lacked prudence. As a leader, I am responsible for people's well-being. As leaders, we must be prudent about our choice of words, our gestures, and even our thoughts. How do we speak with and about people as a leader? Do we speak respectfully, making careful judgments, especially when discussing a third party? Do we accept rumours at face value, or make sure we have the whole story? Do we realize that every word we say as a leader may be taken as gospel truth? Do we use our power to encourage, confirm, and forgive our staff, or to threaten or even humiliate them? How wise the Psalmist's words sound! "Set a guard over my mouth, O Lord; keep watch over the door of my lips" (Psalm 141:3).

We must also be careful about our gestures, our non-verbal communication. Have you ever observed yourself in a mirror, betraying your thoughts and feelings by your facial expression: frowning, opening your eyes wider than usual, pursing your lips, rolling your eyes? Everyone has their own way of expressing feelings non-verbally. Our colleagues and staff are aware of those non-verbal signals. In my community, I recall, it was common knowledge that one had best not enter the office of one particular superior when his cap stood crookedly on his head. No words were necessary! What impression do we leave when we pound on the table, wave our arms, smack our forehead, or make other such gestures? We need to beware of the messages our non-verbal communication sends.

Finally, prudence involves staying calm, not overreacting. Sometimes thoughts or prejudices consume all our energy even before we must take action. How often do we become upset or anxious while preparing for a difficult meeting, simply because we are imagining that the discussion might become unpleasant? Instead, we must try not to get ahead of ourselves. We must take things one step at a time.

It comes down to controlling your own thoughts, and putting a stop to negative ones, because they make us restless and unable to act serenely. I was once told the following story:

> One day, on a quiet road somewhere, a man's car broke down because he had forgotten to put extra gas in it. In the distance, he saw a house where he thought he might find someone who could help him. He started in the direction of the house, but with each step he grew more doubtful. Would they be willing to open the door for him, given the time of night? And if they did open the door, would they be prepared to fill a jerry can with

gas? Some people would refuse, would they not? These days, solidarity is no longer a common thing. And so he started to get all excited, until he arrived at the door and rang, feeling rather angry. Before the man at the door could even ask him in what way he could help him, the driver shouted at him: "Keep your bloody gasoline, if you are not willing to give it to me!"

This story is a good example of where unorganized thoughts may lead.

Experience has taught me that we receive an answer to every problem, and that the best answer may not always be the one I came up with myself.

Courage implies always being willing to go one step further, because we are convinced that by taking the extra step we will attain our objectives. It is risky to oppose prejudices and even advice. Courageous people are not reckless, but they are willing to take calculated and reasonable risks. Leaders must dare to speak their minds, stick out their necks, and react when fundamental values are at stake. Sometimes they must have the courage to remain silent, if the issue cannot be resolved simply by talking about it. Courageous people are usually wise: they know how and when to react, and are always concerned about the well-being of others. They are prepared to give priority to other people's interests, and to suffer if that serves the cause.

It takes courage to make a tough decision, to have an open and honest conversation, to tell the truth without leaving things out. Some decisions may cause pain and hurt, but they are necessary to guarantee the well-being of others in the long term. Courage is required when it comes to admitting mistakes or to acting radically when the organization is functioning poorly due to obstinacy, incompetence, or anger. Courageous are those who treat everyone in the same way and who do not give in to favouritism or to the fear of being criticized. If we speak and act only in order to be cheered or to avoid criticism, we are not serving the cause but rather are defending our own interests, which leads nowhere.

Moderation boils down to using the right measure. The criterion for determining the right measure is the well-being of other people: a good life stimulated through our actions as leader. Keeping measure has to do with our time management, with the use of all kinds of goods, with food and drink. St. Paul encouraged his fellow Christian leaders to be moderate in their consumption of food and drink for good reason: people who know how to keep measure in what they consume will also know what they can ask of their staff and what they cannot. They will not ask so little that the staff might feel underappreciated, and they will not ask so much that the staff might become discouraged or feel that they do not live up to the standards set. Lack of measure is permitted in only one area: love. To quote St. Bernard, the measure of love is its immeasurability.

To conclude our discussion of the quartet of virtues, I wish to add one more thought that should concern ethical leaders these days: ecology. In our attention to people and to the organization, we must not neglect our environment, the earth, which is becoming ever more polluted, exhausted, and overheated. Both in our personal lives and in the lives of our staff, we must place a high priority on ecological issues. We need to respect and protect the environment, use raw materials and energy sources economically, reduce the amount of garbage we produce, and try to keep the air and water as clean as possible. Ethics would be incomplete if the ecological dimension were lacking. As leaders, we must be mindful of the health of our planet – in our words and especially in our actions.

8

I Am Only Human

We lead a team using our whole being. Everyone, though, has weaknesses as well as strengths. We live with this reality as we live from day to day and fulfill our mission.

That people should know and accept themselves is an important general principle. "Know yourself" is an ancient adage; on the basis of that self-knowledge, we can work to develop our strengths and address our weaknesses. Self-knowledge is a long-term process that is never complete. Some dark corners will remain hidden because, consciously or unconsciously, we repress them or because they simply slip from our attention. Obviously, self-knowledge involves a certain amount of effort: the will to really get to know ourselves. Through self-reflection, we analyze our deeds and thoughts, and try to understand our deeper motives.

Fuller self-knowledge also helps in our relationships with others. They hold a mirror before us when they react, make comments, and even reprove us. It is worthwhile to look into that mirror, because there we may discover hidden sides to our personality.

Sometimes we suspect this mirror of reflecting an image that is not true to our nature. For example, a therapy used for treating patients who have anorexia nervosa reveals how difficult it can be to correctly perceive one's own physical appearance. Using a mirror that patients can manipulate themselves, the therapist asks them to shape their reflection according to their true proportions. Most of them are inclined to present themselves as being larger than they actually are. During an exhibition at our museum on the history of psychiatry, we placed such a mirror in one of the rooms. It was remarkable how difficult most people found it to estimate their own dimensions – and these were people who did not have anorexia.

What is true for how we perceive our physical appearance is likely to be equally true, if not more so, for our psychological "appearance." Some people tend to overestimate themselves, believing that they are psychologically strong and well-balanced. Others are inclined to underestimate themselves or constantly doubt their own capacities. The latter group often ends up becoming unable to take action, or else develops compensation mechanisms such as boasting, abuse of power, or a love of material things to hide their insecurity. Indeed, humans are complex beings. The "know yourself" principle is at the same time essential and extremely difficult.

Self-acceptance is important, too. How many people are unhappy because they cannot accept themselves? Judging by the attention people pay to their physical appearance and how many are willing to pay huge amounts of money for plastic surgery, we should not be surprised that many people find it difficult to accept their psychological reality. I suppose it is unrealistic to hope that complete self-acceptance is within reach, but we must work towards such a goal. We lose precious energy by feeling sorry for ourselves, fussing uselessly over characteristics that we have discovered in ourselves, and trying to cover up or gloss over certain elements of our personality.

Refusing to accept ourselves leads to negativism and blocks our possibilities to redirect ourselves more energetically. Non-acceptance prevents the development of a sane kind of self-love, which is necessary if we want to love others as ourselves.

Our leadership, like all other human activities, must always be developed on the basis of self-knowledge, self-acceptance, and self-love. If this foundation is imperfect, then the upper layers will be imperfect as well.

When we are called upon to lead a team, we must continue to pay attention to this foundation. It is a life-long duty. But as we lead a team, we are subject to stimuli that have an effect on the foundation. Praise or encouragement given by our staff will foster our self-acceptance and will render us capable of praising and encouraging others as a way of realizing our love. Reactions from staff members may act as a mirror held before us, helping us to achieve a higher degree of self-knowledge. Failures may discourage us, but they may also become sources of greater self-knowledge, and teach us to estimate our assets and weaknesses more accurately.

Regular evaluation of our leadership may not help us to refine our management style, but it does open doors to rooms of our personality to which we did not have access before. Just as the foundation influences the upper layers, the upper layers have an effect on the foundation. Such interaction is possible only when we quiet ourselves on a regular basis and take time to reflect and assess ourselves. The way we function as leaders will improve, and others will be the first to benefit from this shift.

Through self-knowledge and self-acceptance we will confront our weaknesses. Self-acceptance results in no longer needing to ignore our weaknesses, to struggle against them, or to hide them. We accept them and define them as weaknesses, then set off with them. St. Paul attributed a positive meaning to weaknesses. According to him, our weakness is the place where God prefers to manifest his strength and his grace. As long as we think we're capable of doing everything ourselves, we need neither God's help nor the help of others. What St. Paul explained in a religious sense also has important worldly consequences. When I accept myself as the strong one and deny or hide every weakness, I am claiming that I can accomplish everything on my own, that I do not need anyone's help to accomplish my mission. That kind of attitude is completely opposed to leadership. As leaders, it is and will remain our task to encourage others to use their capacities in order to attain the objectives of the organization together.

Leadership requires that unique combination of strength and weakness. We know that a leader is an important part of the mechanism, but at the same time we realize that many other parts are necessary to make the whole machinery function adequately. The leader had best be the key that starts the machine, knowing when to stay away from where the action takes place, trusting that everyone knows their mission and assumes their responsibilities.

Being able to live with our own weaknesses has yet another consequence. Leaders must have the courage to acknowledge their weaknesses and mistakes. No one is flawless, but contemporary culture no longer tolerates leaders who will not admit it. Political leaders are forced to step down when it becomes known that they have made a mistake and when they are forced to acknowledge that mistake. This kind of mentality causes people to make every possible effort to hide their mistakes, to blame others for what has occurred, or to deny everything. A mistake requires a confession, the opportunity to correct the error or make restitution, and forgiveness. How can we convince young people that they are allowed to make mistakes as long as they learn from them, when we live in and create an atmosphere of perfectionism? It takes courage to admit to a mistake, but doing so clears the path for a more humane kind of leadership and a culture of openness and straightforwardness.

As a leader, I have made mistakes. I am familiar with the desire to cover them up, to hide them, to deny them. But every time I mustered my courage and owned my failings openly, although my pulse quickened, I also experienced a kind of inner peace, as with a catharsis. And time and again, I was surprised by the mildness of my team's reaction, and how they were willing to continue to work towards the realization of our objectives in spite of our errors. To be able to lead a team in an environment where openness and sincerity reign generates a positive energy that, in turn, allows us to keep working towards the goodness of the cause.

Leaders need a sense of humour. Humour helps people to live their lives smiling; serious matters lose their weightiness. Humour makes us take a positive stand in reality and helps us to put ourselves and our situations in perspective. Humour makes the atmosphere more relaxed, and brings people closer to one another; it is a sign that people feel at home in each other's presence. Humour, therefore, is an important tool for leaders. When a leader deals in a humorous way with his staff without becoming over-familiar or cynical or sarcastic, then open and candid communication becomes possible. Not all communication needs to be formal or tense. Real humour becomes possible when people know and appreciate each other. (To keep humour healthy and life-giving, do not dilute it with anger; humour becomes cynicism or sarcasm when a certain degree of bitterness is involved.)

Humour is important in our relationship with ourselves, as well: sometimes we need to be able to laugh at ourselves. We must put ourselves into perspective, to see beyond the weightiness of our function, to refuse to get caught in and become the victim of our function. We are all familiar with leaders who seem to live their lives weighed down by the heavy cross of responsibility, and who become tense whenever their leadership is the subject of discussion. The combination of humour and leadership is the result of a sufficient amount of self-confidence and the capacity to maintain a realistic perspective on ourselves. Only when we find this balance will we feel free in our function and avoid stress. Humour is a real art that renders life pleasant and that deserves to be cultivated.

The topic of perspective brings us to time management. Leaders and managers are invited to develop both their personal and professional lives in a well-balanced and sane way through proper use of the time accorded to them. They should be able to start and stop work on time, and to organize everything within the normal deadlines, giving priority to the most important activities and ensuring that the latter are not postponed due to unforeseen circumstances.

Good time management requires a clear agenda for the day in which opening, transitional, and closing rituals have a place. How we start the day can determine the atmosphere throughout our workday. Take your time as you start the day so that peacefulness may characterize the rest of it. Begin daily duties by planning them one by one, and make sure that priorities remain priorities! In our day and age, we often let the order of the day be determined by incoming email and telephone calls. This approach is risky, as our focus can shift from acting to reacting. Obviously, it is impossible to postpone all unforeseen requests and questions. We must provide enough time in our daily agenda to meet an unexpected visitor or have a necessary conversation.

In determining priorities, we must make sure that they tally with our mission as leader. Several good techniques are available to attune our activities to the mission of the company or organization.

During the day, provide a number of pauses: enjoy a meal, take a walk, or have a nap. Some people allow for a moment of reflection so they can concentrate again.

Sane time management implies stopping work on time. Working overtime on a regular basis leaves us fatigued and unable to fulfill our other duties and obligations. At the end of each day, assess yourself, write in your journal, review the day, and prepare for tomorrow. Nervous exhaustion and burnout can be attributed to poor time management, which causes managers to exhaust all their energy early on in their careers. Everyone has their own way of replenishing their energy. Identifying which techniques work for you requires self-knowledge and self-acceptance, too.

We lead a team as humans who have certain capacities, but also certain limitations. This is what makes our leadership so human.

9

Christ-inspired Leadership

We began our reflection on leadership with the observation that leadership is impossible without a spiritual foundation. I wish to conclude this reflection with a discussion of how Christianity offers a model for leadership that is life-giving and timeless. I find my own inspiration in Christianity, the figure of Jesus Christ, and the teachings of the Gospel. These sources influence my thoughts and actions, and so give shape to my leadership style. Given these Christian roots, I think we can talk about a Christ-inspired leadership.

What is Christ-inspired leadership?

This type of leadership draws us to the figure of Jesus Christ, our model, and the way he played his role as a leader. For Jesus, to lead was to serve. He refused to be called master or rabbi, showing that the leader's rightful place is at the feet of his followers. The night before he died, he literally washed the feet of his disciples during the Last Supper, and proclaimed that the disciples were to do the same for others. "Whoever wishes to become great among you must be your servant" (Matthew 20:26). Through this paradox, he stressed the importance of service. That is why service has become one of the primary features of Christianity and thus of Christ-inspired leadership.

Of a servant leader, we expect dedication to the well-being of others and a willingness to take this dedication to the extreme. In Christ's case, the servant leader sacrificed his life for others.

I continue to be moved by the actions of former Russian President Mikhail Gorbachev, who, by introducing the idea of *perestroika* or restructuring, called the entire communist system into question and ultimately undermined it; in the end, he was forced to resign. This was the price that this servant-leader had to pay, and, it seems, was willing to pay.

In the modern literature on the topic, this point of view is reiterated by Robert Greenleaf. In 1970, he published a small book entitled *The Servant as Leader*. In describing the servant leader, he says,

> The servant-leader is servant first. It begins with the natural feeling that one wants to serve. Then conscious choice brings one to aspire to lead. The best test is: do those served grow as persons; do they, while being served, become healthier, wiser, freer, more autonomous, more likely themselves to become servants? (p. 13)

Greenleaf secularized the Christian view on the leadership of service and proved its universal value. Since that time, over half a million copies of Greenleaf's books on leadership have been sold.

To my mind, the aspect of service is inherent to any kind of leadership. If it is absent, the leadership might become seriously misdirected. To paraphrase Gaillot, we might say, "If serving is not the leader's purpose, then he or she serves no purpose at all." Leaders who do not serve their employees and cause probably serve other masters, beginning with themselves, and strive for power and money. This behaviour may end in a serious misuse of authority, thanks to which the leader may accumulate even more power and money.

Christian leaders are doubly dependent. They are at the service of others and at the service of the Lord. In other words, God gives them a mandate to become the servant of other people. This aspect adds a special angle to the project of leading a team. The project is no longer understood to be a personal one, wherein leaders are to realize themselves. The result is often exhaustion, and an attempt to constantly prove themselves, which legitimizes their leadership with their own boss as well as their staff. Leadership that is based on Christ's example invites us to imitate Christ: in our work, we hope to fulfill God's mission, God's will, God's calling. We receive a mandate and are given the strength to accomplish that mission, thanks to the grace of God.

My own experience is a testimony to the truth of this statement. Through my relationship with God, I receive the strength each day to carry out my role as leader. Does this depreciate my own strength, my own competence, my own dedication? No – on the contrary. Through God's grace, my strength, my competence, and my dedication grow and are stimulated internally. God uses me as an instrument to build his kingdom on earth. And to that purpose, God requires a good instrument: competent, diligent, and dedicated. Christian leaders freely declare themselves willing to serve others. They do not assume a position above their staff, in order to impose their own will and their own demands. No. They make the objectives of the organization their own and promote them with their staff. Their authority consists in inviting, motivating, building a sense of community, and concretizing the mission.

Christian leaders must be both humble and meek. They must be aware of their place as servants and know that their leadership can be realized only in an atmosphere of meekness. This approach differs dramatically from that of many contemporary leaders, who surround themselves with symbols of their power, creating an atmosphere of aloofness. They are drunk on their power and excel at taking themselves seriously. They gather around them a group of people who, in order to defend their own interests, fulfill but one task: safeguarding the leader's prestige and standing. We have seen the results of such a system. We know that the consequences can be disastrous for the organization and even the nation when that kind of leader is in charge.

On the subject of humility, I am always reminded of Jesus' mother, Mary. When she is visited by the Angel Gabriel, she refers to herself as the Lord's humble handmaiden. But her meekness and humility are not like those of someone who is fearful or weak. She knows that great things are possible, thanks to the strength she has received from above. Her Magnificat, where she proclaims the greatness of the Lord, and her whole life bear witness to this attitude. Such is the humility that may be expected of leaders: in the One who gives me strength, I can accomplish great things.

Christian leaders also strive for the ideal that is God, who at the same time *"ordonne, donne et pardonne"* (gives orders, gives power, and grants forgiveness). This wonderful image from Belgian Cardinal Danneels touches me deeply. God proclaims his commandments clearly and asks us to live according to them. God gives us the power to live by those commandments through his grace. And God grants forgiveness when we fail. Christian leaders should follow God's example, seeking inspiration for their leadership in that triad of activities. They, too, must prod and encourage people to fulfill the objectives of the organization. When leaders only give orders, but fail to take other steps to motivate, their performance is inadequate. Many leaders give clear guidelines, draw up procedures, and expect their staff to follow these guidelines to the letter. Those who cannot follow them or who make mistakes are let go, because they slow down the organization. After giving humankind the Ten Commandments, God sent prophets, and eventually his own Son, to guide the people, to encourage them, to give them the strength to obey the Law. Good leaders in our day do the same: they give staff different insights, teach them to look at things from fresh angles, help them begin their tasks, and perhaps accompany them through these tasks. God is a charitable and merciful Father, who keeps forgiving, offering humanity chance upon chance to make up for its faults. As leaders, we can follow God's example.

Love is the greatest among the virtues. Without love, we are nothing, as St. Paul says (1 Corinthians 13:2). When an element of love is lacking in our leadership, I fear that it will be harsh. As someone once wrote,

> Duty without love leads to doggedness;
> Responsibility without love leads to mercilessness;
> Justice without love leads to harshness;
> Truth without love leads to criticalness;
> Smartness without love leads to cunning;
> Kindness without love leads to hypocrisy;
> Order without love leads to narrow-mindedness;
> Honour without love leads to haughtiness;
> Property without love leads to avariciousness;
> Faith without love leads to fanaticism;
> Life without love is meaningless.

We find a number of helpful guidelines in Scripture. St. Paul addresses the topic in his Letter to Timothy.

> Now a bishop must be above reproach, married only once, temperate, sensible, respectable, hospitable, an apt teacher, not a drunkard, not violent but gentle, not quarrelsome, and not a lover of money. He must manage his own household well, keeping his children submissive and respectful in every way .... (1 Timothy 3:2-4)

This list of characteristics bears witness to a profound knowledge of humankind and to a high degree of humanity. These attitudes still have great value today. Leaders, according to St. Paul's model, are people who can control themselves and who have pure intentions concerning their task; they are generous, not avaricious.

If we intend to take the Gospel as a whole as a guideline for leadership, we must pay attention to the great values of the Sermon on the Mount (see Matthew chapters 5 to 7):

> Blessed are the poor in spirit, for theirs is the kingdom of heaven.
>
> Blessed are those who mourn, for they will be comforted.
>
> Blessed are the meek, for they will inherit the earth.
>
> Blessed are those who hunger and thirst for righteousness, for they will be filled.
>
> Blessed are the merciful, for they will receive mercy.
>
> Blessed are the pure in heart, for they will see God.
>
> Blessed are the peacemakers, for they will be called children of God.
>
> Blessed are those who are persecuted for righteousness' sake, for theirs is the kingdom of heaven.

Blessed are you when people revile you and persecute you and utter all kinds of evil against you falsely on my account. Rejoice and be glad, for your reward is great in heaven, for in the same way they persecuted the prophets who were before you.

These values are fruits of the Holy Spirit: love, joy, peace, patience, kindness, goodness, trust, meekness, and self-control (see Galatians 5:22-23). Let us examine each of them, considering their relevance in our day and age.

Leadership should be marked by *joy*, and a leader should foster feelings of joy. Joy is a gift that people receive when they see all things good, true, and beautiful grow within them and around them.

Leaders should also promote *peace*. They should be able to create an atmosphere of harmony in a group, helping the group to transcend its differences. I do not refer to the kind of peace whereby everyone and everything is left in peace, and changes are avoided in the name of peace. That is a false kind of peace, the kind that Jesus said he would not bring.

Leaders should be *patient*, for the staff's tempo is not always their own. Thinking of the expression "grass doesn't grow faster when you pull at it," I encourage leaders to respect the natural growth process, to give people time to integrate changes, and to believe that actions taken today may yield results only at a much later date. Then, like the Dutch poet Adriaan Roland Holst, we can confidently say, "I will not see the corn-stalks, neither will I put them in sheaves, but make me believe in the harvest for which I serve …."

There is no need for me to explain how important it is to be truly *kind* to staff, as a sign of your deep respect for them. Staff can accomplish much more when they are treated kindly rather than coldly and grumpily. Kindness must be sincere, however, or it becomes perverted.

Being good to others involves considering what the staff members are dealing with, making sure that justice prevails. Goodness has everything to do with justice.

When leaders put their *trust* in their staff, the staff will trust in their leaders. Where distrust predominates, staff will conceal things from management. This behaviour leads to hidden agendas and results in serious dissatisfaction. When a leader attempts to keep control only by introducing all kinds of mechanisms, but ignores a fundamental lack of trust, staff will develop just as many alternative mechanisms to escape that supervision and control. Trust, meanwhile, generates more trust.

Some leaders believe that raising their voices will show their staff who is boss, who's in charge. However, by shouting, by getting angry or bitter, a leader demonstrates fear and insecurity. Leaders who are at peace with themselves, who relay messages calmly without raising their voices, show that they are *meek* and in control of their affairs. They should avoid making remarks when they are under pressure, angry, or aware of aggressive feelings. They do better to wait until they have calmed down before giving their message.

Self-control consists of being able to transcend emotions; it is a combination of patience, meekness, and peace. Only when people are again at peace with themselves, which involves being patient, can they approach the other meekly and kindly.

These fruits of the Holy Spirit can never be the result of our own efforts alone. We must pray for them, opening up to God's love, and God's grace will then give us the strength we need to shape our leadership.

Let that be our conclusion. Let us hope that we may become good leaders, serving others, thanks to our own informed efforts and the power of God's grace.

This book has been printed on 100% post consumer waste paper, certified Eco-logo and processed chlorine free.